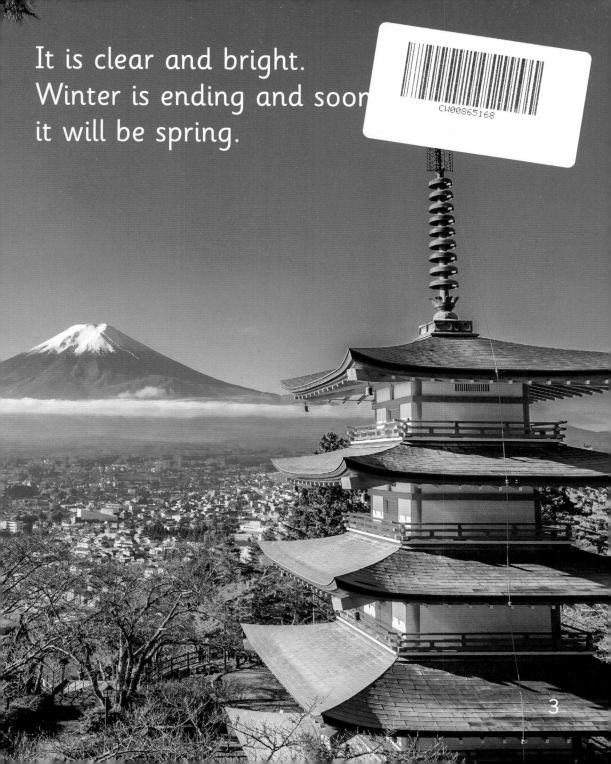

It is clear and bright.
Winter is ending and soon
it will be spring.

In spring, clusters of bright buds start to appear on the trees.

4

Flowers bloom and transform the parks and streets. Boats float down the river.

In summer, children finish school.
They swim at the coast to cool down.

There is fresh fish and shrimp for lunch.
Children scoop it up with spoons
or chopsticks.

In September, the trees turn from green to bright red and brown. The air is crisp and cool.

High winds and storms start blustering.
Rain sweeps in from the coast.

It is now winter, and children speed down steep hills.

Hundreds of bright lights appear across the hills, floating in the darkness.

The year is ending. The crowded streets are hectic with lots of shoppers.

The next year starts with bells and sweet foods. Spring will begin again soon.

A year in Japan

After reading

Letters and Sounds: Phase 4

Word count: 167

Focus on adjacent consonants with long vowel phonemes, e.g. /t/ /r/ /ai/ /n/

Common exception words: of, to, the, are, they, there, school

Curriculum links: Geography: Place knowledge, Human and physical geography

National Curriculum learning objectives: Reading/word reading: apply phonic knowledge and skills as the route to decode words; Reading/comprehension: understand ... books they can already read accurately and fluently ... by drawing on what they already know or on background information and vocabulary provided by the teacher

Developing fluency

- Your child may enjoy hearing you read the book.
- You could take turns to each read a page.

Phonic practice

- Support your child to practise reading two- and three-syllable words.
- Ask your child to:
  - o Sound talk and blend each syllable "chunk".
  - o Then read each chunk to read the whole word.

  trans/form   chop/sticks   Sep/tem/ber   win/ter

  - o Now read the words quickly without chunking them.

Extending vocabulary

- Ask your child to spot the synonyms below (they may need help reading some words). Which is the odd one out?

1. ending	beginning	finish	(*beginning*)
2. busy	hectic	quiet	(*quiet*)
3. drop	scoop	lift	(*drop*)
4. appear	show	end	(*end*)